Thoughts On Life and Godliness

THOUGHTS

ON

LIFE AND GODLINESS.

" His Divine power hath given unto us all things that pertain unto life and godliness."—2 Pet. i. 3.

BY THE

Rev. EVAN H. HOPKINS,

Vicar of Holy Trinity, Richmond, Surrey.

LONDON:

HODDER & STOUGHTON,

27, PATERNOSTER ROW.

1878.

LONDON :

BARRETT, SONS AND CO., PRINTERS,

SEETHING LANE.

CONTENTS.

THOUGHTS

ON

LIFE AND GODLINESS.

~~~~~~

Walking with God.

"Enoch walked with God."—*Gen.* v. 24.

"By faith Enoch was translated that he should not see death: and was not found, because God had translated him: for before his translation he had this testimony that he pleased God."—*Heb.* xi. 5.

WHEN we think of Enoch, we think of a man eminent for his holiness. Very little is said about him; but how much is comprehended in that one short sentence, he "walked with God." How many are the thoughts suggested by these words!

B

I. A WAY.—Not an *entrance* merely, not a *door* through which we have to enter, but a *road*. Not a *point* to which we have to come, but a *line* along which we are to travel. Salvation is a way. Salvation is all the way — a path leading right up to glory. So David said not only, "Thou hast brought me up out of the horrible pit, and set my feet upon a rock," but "Thou hast established my *goings*" (Ps. xl. 2). Here, then, we have not a footing only, but a way. "Enoch *walked* with God." Another thought suggested by the words is

II. PROGRESS.—The Scriptures frequently put this truth before us. Is the believer compared to a *tree*? Then he is to *grow*— in the root, in the branches. Is the Church compared to a building? Then we read that "all the building, fitly framed together, *groweth*" (Eph. ii. 21). Or to a body? Then that the whole body, fitly joined together and compacted, "maketh *increase*"

(Eph. iv. 16). So here we have the thought of progress—advancement.

But let us mark the *manner* of the progress. It is *walking*. Not limping, or crawling, or moving along like one who is lame. Many things hinder our walking, and these hindrances are illustrated in the miracles wrought by Christ. There was a man brought to our Lord who could *not walk*—he was sick of the palsy. The first word our Lord spake to him was "Son, thy sins be forgiven thee." But those who stood by thought nothing of this. It was when Jesus had said, "Arise, take up thy bed, and *walk*," and the man obeying, that the people were amazed, and glorified God, and said, "We never saw it on this fashion." So let us remember, if we have pardon, the world cannot *see* the forgiveness of our sins. But let us obey Christ's command, Arise and walk, and then they will not only be astonished, they will glorify our Father who is in heaven. Look at another example (Luke

xiii. 11)—the woman with a spirit of infirmity eighteen years, and who was bowed together, and could in nowise lift up herself. Walking implies an upright, erect attitude; but here was one who was bent down. Are there not many Christians who, though they are in the right road, are not in a true attitude? Jesus *saw* her, *called* her, *spoke* to her, and *laid His hands* on her, and she was made *straight* and glorified God. So if we are really *walking* with God we shall lift up our face unto Him (Job. xxii. 26).

But there are others again who are hindered walking, because, like Lazarus, they are *bound*. They have heard the voice of Jesus saying "Come forth," but they need the words "Loose him, and let him go." They have life, but they need *liberty*. Here, then, are some of the hindrances to our progress—to our *walking* with God. Some are sick, some are bowed down, some are bound with grave-clothes: and then there are those whose limbs are *out of joint*. The Apostle prayed for the Hebrew converts, " The God of peace, make you perfect "—put you into joint— " in every good work to do His will." So long as the limb is dislocated progress will be a hard and painful process; and so, many Christians tell us it is. But *walking* is an *easy*, *healthy*, and *pleasant* exercise. It should not be toil, but liberty. " My yoke is easy, and my burden is light." This is true in experience only when the will and the affections are in harmony with God; if the machinery is out of gear how can it work smoothly?

" Enoch walked *with* God." " He that is not *with* Me is against Me." Here we have

III. FRIENDSHIP.—" Can two walk *together* except they be agreed?" They may walk in the same road—one following a long way after the other, as Peter followed Jesus afar off; but they cannot walk *together.* What does it mean? Identity of desires, of feelings, of objects; the same joys, the same aims. This leads to

IV. COMMUNION.—" *With God* "—intercourse between the soul and God. God speaks to us, through His word. We speak to Him, in prayer. To walk with God does not mean walking *to* the light, but *in* the light, and *abiding* in it. And lastly there is

V. FELLOWSHIP.—This is more than Friendship, or Intercourse, or Communion. It is Partnership with God. It is more—it is *Participation of God.* "Partakers of the Divine Nature." To have, not only His Favour—but His Life. Not merely the life that He gives, but *the life that He lives.* The life of God in the soul. It is to this we are called—" unto the fellowship of His Son Jesus Christ our Lord " (1 Cor. i. 9). When you received Christ, you received Him in whom " *all fulness* dwells." God has called you to a participation of that fulness.

Let us look at a *prayer* and a *promise* bearing on this wonderful subject of " Walking with God "—

Ps. lvi. 13 : " For Thou hast delivered my *soul* from *death :* wilt not Thou deliver my *feet* from *falling*, that I may *walk* before God in the light of the living?" Observe the ground we are privileged to occupy as believers in the Lord Jesus. We can say, "Thou *hast* delivered my soul from death." Salvation, so far as justification and acceptance are concerned, is a completed thing. We have been saved from death—we are passed from death unto life (John v. 24). And, moreover, Christ in glory is our standing; as He is, so are we in this world, in God the Father's sight. With what confidence then may we pray, "Deliver my feet from falling, that I may *walk*." We have received the greatest blessing (*soul* from *death*), may we not confidently expect the lesser mercy (*feet* from *falling*—sliding back)? And for our encouragement He has given us a promise—

John viii. 12: "I am the light of the world: he that followeth Me shall not walk in darkness, but shall have the light of life." When Jesus says, "I *am*," we must think not so much of His *gifts* as of *Himself*. Is it light

we need on our way? Then He says, " I AM
the light." And what does He promise?
Freedom from darkness. To be living in
any known sin is to be in darkness. To be
walking in uncertainty as to our acceptance
with God, or as to whether we please Him, is
to be in darkness. To be spending our days
in gloom and sadness is to be in darkness.
But Jesus says I shall *not* walk in darkness.
If then to-day I am in darkness, there must
be something wrong somewhere; not in His
Word, His precious promise, but in me, in
my experience. And what is the cause?
This blessing is conditional. " He that *followeth* Me." It is not enough that I have
"*come*" to Him; I must "*follow*," I must
"*abide*" in Him. If I am really following
Him—walking with God—I shall not abide
in darkness. I shall find the truth of these
words in Proverbs iv. 18, in my own experience: "The path of the just is as the
shining light, that shineth more and more
unto the perfect day." There are various

readings of that passage, which man has invented. One is, "The path of the just is as the shining light, which shineth more or *less* unto the perfect day." But God has written "*more and* MORE." The path then will shine brighter as we follow Him; freedom from sin, from uncertainty, and from gloom. But this is not all; this is but the negative side of the blessing, "*He shall have the light of life.*" He shall have it as a *possession.* Christ Himself, who first shone *on* him, will shine *in* him. "In Him was life; and the life was the *light* of men" (John i. 4).

Oh to walk so that we do not hinder His shining! If we *walk with God*, we shall walk humbly, watchfully, prayerfully.

The Law of Liberty.

THE *ground* upon which God deals with us is GRACE. Every blessing we receive of Him as His children is undeserved. From the beginning to the end of our whole spiritual existence we are debtors to the rich, free, sovereign grace of God.

And what is it we are privileged to enjoy on that ground, when we enter "into this grace wherein we stand?" We then have a new *position*, and that position is CHRIST. We are not only pardoned but justified—made righteous; and this not merely by that which Christ has *done*, or by what He has procured or bestows—but *in* that which He *is*. The *ground* the believer occupies is *grace*, the *position* he enjoys is *Christ*. God regards him now in Christ, and as Christ. "As He is, so are we in this world." (1 John iv. 17.)

The believer must never lose sight of this fundamental truth, and that the *basis* of his communion with God is not his own personal holiness, or what Christ is *in* him, but his judicial position before God, or what Christ is *for* him. Christ as "the Lord our Righteousness" is the foundation of everything — of walk as well as of standing.

But besides the ground on which he stands, and the position he enjoys, the believer must recognise the *laws* by which his spiritual life is governed.

The Apostle says in Rom. viii. 2 : "The *law* of the spirit of life in Christ Jesus hath made me free from the *law* of sin and death."

What do we understand by a law? A certain fixed principle, something which in its working has all the certainty, regularity, and force of a law.

There are the laws of *nature*. As, for instance, the law of gravitation. We know that this is a principle which nothing can change—it is fixed and unalterable. Our natural life is regulated by that law. We cannot do anything contrary to it without feeling the consequences.

So there are laws of *grace*, of a man's spiritual being.

And there is "the law of sin and death"— that principle of evil which sinks the soul down, and causes it to depart from God. That is a law which can never be changed. Sin and corruption can no more lose their tendency to drag the soul downward, than a lump of lead can be made to lose its weight, or the tendency to gravitate to the earth's centre. And yet that piece of lead may be caused to ascend by bringing another law into operation which has just the opposite tendency. Fasten it to a balloon, and, instead of sinking or falling, it will rise.

Again, if a man is thrown into the sea, by the law of gravitation he sinks to the bottom. But put a life-belt round him, and by another law—the law of floating bodies—he floats on the surface. The two laws remain as they

were, they are neither changed nor destroyed
—both are in operation, but the stronger overcomes the other.

So it is in the life of faith. As the law of
sin and death sinks the soul downwards,
so "the law of the spirit of life in Christ
Jesus" raises the soul upwards. Which is
the stronger?

The life-belt is provided that the man who
without it would sink—*may* not sink. So
"the Spirit of life in Christ Jesus" is given
that the soul who, because of the flesh within,
must sink and depart from God, need not
sin but abide in the light. "And these are
contrary the one to the other."

As the power that keeps the man afloat is
against or opposed to the force that would
sink him to the bottom, so the " Spirit (tend-
eth) against the flesh," in order "that ye
may not do the things that ye would."

"The law of the Spirit of life in Christ
Jesus hath made me *free* from the law of sin
and death." What freedom is this? Free-

dom not from the presence, or *inbeing* of sin,
but from the dominion, or *service* of sin.
The Apostle is referring to the bondage he
alluded to in chapter vi. 12, 16, 20, " Let not
sin therefore *reign*," &c. Do not *serve* sin, do
not *obey* it. See also chapter vii. 5, 6, 14,
23. It is not only freedom from the guilt but
from the *dominion* of sin. It is the freedom
we need, not for a justified *state* only, but for
a holy and consistent *walk*.

But this freedom does not imply that the
tendency of evil within us is destroyed. Although, by means of the life-belt, the man is
kept floating above the waters so that he is
not drowned, he is not thereby freed from the
force of gravitation, he is only freed from its
overcoming power. So the believer, although
he is freed from the necessity of *obeying* "the
law of sin," which would sink him into transgression, " by the law of the Spirit of life in
Christ Jesus," he is not thereby freed from the
constant influence or tendency of the flesh to
drag him down. Sin's force is not destroyed;
though by virtue of the Spirit's power it is

rendered ineffectual. The believer, though not free from the presence and constant influence of sin, is free from its *dominion*.

No one can disregard the laws of nature without suffering the consequences. Those laws must be respected and obeyed. So the laws of God's spiritual kingdom must be obeyed. And as Bacon says, "He who obeys Nature commands her."

If the man leaves the life-belt—no matter how long he may have floated—he sinks as easily at the end as he did at the beginning. So the believer must not presume on past experience or grace received. He needs to abide in Christ every moment—this very moment as much as when, years ago, it may be, he first came to Jesus. The law of sin is the same to-day as it was then. On the other hand, as the man who remains in the life-belt enjoys all the power and force of one of God's unalterable laws by which the universe is governed, and in virtue of that law is preserved from sinking—not by struggling but by abiding, not by his own efforts to keep himself afloat, but by casting himself upon the life-belt to do it—so the believer that "abides in Christ" enjoys, whilst he thus abides, all the power of one of God's immutable laws by which His spiritual kingdom is governed; and in virtue of that law the believer is preserved from being brought under the dominion of evil—not by struggling but by abiding, not by his own efforts not to sink, but by casting himself implicitly upon Christ to keep him from sinking.

The one is not more certain than the other. God's laws of grace are as fixed and reliable as God's laws of nature. How important we should understand them, recognise them, and obey them.

"Walk in the Spirit, and ye shall *not fulfil* the lust of the flesh" (Gal. v. 16.)

"There is, therefore, now no condemnation to them which are in Christ Jesus. For the law of the Spirit of life in Christ Jesus HATH MADE ME FREE from the law of sin and death."

Living in the Name of the Lord.

" THE name of the Lord " is a phrase
that occurs very frequently in the
word of God. It is a phrase with which
we are so familiar that we are in danger of
overlooking its full meaning.

In Proverbs xviii. 10 we read, for instance,
" The name of the Lord is a strong tower:
the righteous runneth into it, and is safe."
We have contemplated Christ in that aspect,
chiefly, perhaps, in reference to the sinner
fleeing for mercy. We have ourselves re-
joiced in Him as our Refuge from the penalty
of sin, and have found in Him safety, rest
and peace.

But is not the passage especially applicable
to the child of God? Although it contains
the truth of primary importance to the sin-
convicted soul, it really describes the privilege

c

of the "righteous." It tells us what the
child of God is privileged to do in reference
to that name,—he *runs into it ;* and what
he invariably finds when he thus runs into
it,—he is *safe*, that is, *delivered* from whatever evil may then assail him.

The whole Gospel is summed up in God's
names. To proclaim the glad tidings, and
to declare the name of the Lord, are one and
the same thing. Moses prayed, " I beseech
Thee show me Thy glory." God answered,
" I will proclaim the *name* of the Lord before
thee." Standing in the cleft of the rock, and
covered with the hand of the Lord, Moses
heard that name proclaimed—" The Lord,
the Lord God, merciful and gracious, longsuffering and abundant in forgiveness and
truth, keeping mercy for thousands, forgiving
iniquity, transgression and sin." There we
have a revelation of God's character—an unfolding of Jehovah's name. So, again, in the
Law, what have we but a manifestation of
the name of the Lord ? In the moral law we

see shining forth the rays of His holiness, justice and truth. Not a full transcript of God's character it is true, because the revelation was but partial, but, so far as it went, it showed what God was; it set forth His name.

So too, in the ceremonial law, we see God's name declared. Every sacrifice, as it met some special side of man's need, revealed at the same time some special aspect of God's character, some special view of His name, as the God of grace, of righteousness, of mercy, and of truth. And yet all these Old Testament revelations were but imperfect manifestations of Jehovah's name. They were fragmentary in substance and manifold in form. As we read in Heb. i. 1, " God, who at sundry times and in divers manners spake unto the fathers by the prophets " (*i.e.*, God who in *many parts*, not in one undivided whole, but in part ; and in *many ways* revealed His name to the Old Testament saints), " has in these last days spoken unto us by His Son." In Christ the revelation of God is not partial

or imperfect, but full and complete—not in
part but as a glorious whole. And He could
say, "Father, I have declared Thy name."
"I have manifested Thy name." The whole
life of Christ was a revelation of God's name.
He was "the brightness of the Father's glory
and the express image of His person."

But our God and Saviour has many names.
Just as our needs are many, so His names
are manifold. For every need in self there
is a Divine name, into which we may run
and find deliverance.

"The name of the Lord is a strong tower."
A *tower*. Consider the end and use of a
tower in a besieged city. When all the out-
posts are taken, the walls scaled, the fortifications forsaken, the houses left, it is to the
tower that the people flee.

So when all Satan's legions surround thee,
when the powers of darkness encompass thy
soul, and thou art driven from all other places
of refuge, then think of the name of the Lord.
"Who is among you that feareth the Lord,

that obeyeth the voice of His servant, that walketh in darkness, and hath no light ? Let him trust *in the name of the Lord*, and stay upon his God." " Thou art my hiding-place."
. God's name is a " *strong* tower"—an impregnable fortress. It not only gives immediate shelter, it affords eternal security. When a man is in a tower the walls are around him; on every side he is protected. So when the soul trusts in the name of the Lord he is garrisoned in all the attributes of the unchanging Jehovah. He is safe. In the margin it is, he is " set aloft"; that is, lifted up above the reach of his foes. The shafts of the enemy can do him no harm.

Let God's children remember these words in their daily trials. No matter what may be the nature of your difficulties, temptations, conflicts, perplexities, there is revealed in God's Holy Word just the name you need to meet your every emergency. Are you tempted to give way to sin ?—remember His name. He is called JESUS to *save* you *from* your

sins. Run into that name by a definite act
of trust, and He will be to you at that
moment of danger a strong tower, and you
shall be saved from falling into sin.

Let us be ever learning the names of Christ.
He has many names. How many do you
know,—not intellectually, merely, but spiritually, practically, experimentally ? As you
advance, as you are enabled to overcome, so
you will be learning Christ more and more.
in all His wondrous names. And the fulfil-
ment of that promise will be yours : " To
him that overcometh will I give to eat of the
hidden manna, and I will give him a white
stone " (*i.e.* the same testimony that Enoch
had, that he pleased God), "and in the stone
a new name written " (not a new name given
to the believer, but a new *name of Christ*
revealed to the believer), "which no man
knoweth saving he that receiveth it." (Com-
pare Rev. iii. 12, "*my* new name.")

Here, again, is the secret of all acceptable
service and all true testimony. It must be
in the name as well as *about* the name of the

Lord that he has to bear witness. Hence it
is written, in Matt. x. 32 : "Whosoever,
therefore, shall confess Me before men"—
literally, "confess *in* Me" (ἐν ἐμοί). "This
corresponds with the idea of ἐν χριστῷ εἶναι."
"The ἐν is not equivalent to '*in behalf of me*,'
but it shows the ground or root of the confession, namely, a living union with Christ."
(*Lange.*)

But some may say, "How can I remember
all His names, and the *special* Name I need
at the time?" Let the need itself suggest the
name. Weakness will suggest His strength,
emptiness His fulness, unrest His peace.
Christ has as many names as we have needs.

How instructive is this truth in connection
with the life of Abraham. In the twelfth
chapter of Genesis, God revealed Himself
to Abraham as a God of *blessing*. In the
fifteenth chapter we have another manifestation of the Divine name: "Fear not, Abram ;
I am thy *shield*, and thy exceeding great *reward*." What is a shield? A covering—a
protection—the soul's first need. "Behold

our shield, and look upon the face of thine
anointed." It is as such we first trusted in
Christ. Under Him, as our Shield, we find
security and rest. Jehovah was also his
"reward." That pointed to the future. So
Christ is our present shelter and our glorious
hope. Then, in Gen. xvii. 1, God reveals
Himself under a new name :—"I am the
Almighty God "—*El Shaddai.* That is, the
God of all sufficiency—of infinite power, and
boundless provision—able to fulfil all His
promises, and to deliver from all enemies.
Hence the command, "Walk before Me and
be thou perfect "—upright, free from blame—
was not a grievous requirement to Abram, if
only he lived by faith in that name. For in
this new name he had not only the security
(in the shield) and the prospect (in the reward) he had the present provision for every
need, in the name *El Shaddai.* And so it
has pleased the Father that all fulness should
dwell in Christ for His children. "Walk ye
in Him."

The Things of Faith.

THERE are the things of *sense*, the things of *fancy*, and the things of *faith*. The first pertain to our feelings and emotions, the second to our imagination, the third to the invisible realities revealed to us in the Word of God. The things of faith may be distinguished from the things of sense by the fact that they are "things not seen" by natural perception; and from the things of fancy by the fact that they have an actual existence. We know that the things of sense have a being from the evidence of sight, or touch, or hearing, as the case may be. And we know that the things of faith have an actual existence from the testimony of Scripture; we know it by faith, which is not only "the substance"—foundation, or ground of confidence—"of things hoped for," but the "evidence" or proof, "of things not seen." But the things of fancy have no substance, no foundation. What the senses are to the body, or to the "outward man" faith is to the "inward man." We are persuaded of the presence of a visible object when we see it; so we are assured of the reality of some spiritual fact when we believe it. And the warrant of our believing it is the testimony of Scripture.

By keeping these distinctions in mind we shall be enabled to guard against two evils—the ever-changing, miserable up-and-down life of *feeling*, on the one hand; and the uncertain and dangerous course of *fanaticism*, on the other. The true path is the path of *faith*, which is always on the ground of Divine testimony, and "shineth *more and more* unto the perfect day."

Faith has to do with things "hoped for" —the promises of God (future)—and with "things not seen"—the facts (past and present) revealed in God's Word. Let us now consider some of the things of faith presented to us in the New Testament.

I.—THE "RIGHTEOUSNESS OF FAITH."

This is the first thing we must know. It is the first, both in order and in importance. If we are wrong here, we are wrong altogether. What is the righteousness in which you seek to be accepted before God? There is only one righteousness that can justify us in His sight, and that is the "righteousness of God." And yet how many are deluded with the idea that their own works may contribute to this righteousness! It is the righteousness of God (Rom. iii. 21, 22), because God has provided it; because Christ Himself is made of God unto us righteousness (1 Cor. i. 30), and is called "the Lord our Righteousness" (Jer. xxiii. 6). It is the "righteousness of *Faith*," because it is "unto all and upon all them that *believe*" (Rom. iii. 22); we receive it, not by working, or feeling, or realising, or supposing, but simply by *believing*. Let us never lose sight of this fundamental truth of our religion, but ever keep in mind the Apostle's great aim and desire "that I may be found in Him" (*i.e.* Christ), "not having mine own righteousness, which is of the law, but that which is through the faith of Christ, the righteousness which is of God *by faith*" (Phil. iii. 9).

II.—THE "JOY OF FAITH" (Phil. i. 25).

The kingdom of God is not meat and drink; but righteousness, and peace, and *joy* in the Holy Ghost" (Rom. xiv. 17). It is a Divine command that we "*Rejoice* in the Lord *alway*" (Phil. iv. 4), and when God says "alway" He does not mean sometimes merely. And yet how impossible this seems to many Christians! Simply because they confound the things of sense, of feeling, with the things of faith. Rejoicing in the Lord is the "joy of faith"—a joy arising, not from outward circumstances and inward emotions, but from certain spiritual realities apprehended by faith. The believer's heart is often gladdened by the outward and manifest blessings which God pours out upon him. There is the joy of Christian fellowship; the joy of seeing souls brought to the Saviour; the joy of being made useful in His vineyard. But these are not strictly the things of *faith*. They have passed into another sphere, so to speak. We first receive God's gifts by faith. We believe in their reality, we accept them, and we act *as if we saw and felt them*, because we take God's testimony as equivalent to the testimony of our senses. But when the promises, which we received and obtained by faith, are fulfilled, so as to be present to our senses, then they pass out of the sphere of faith into the region of realisation, of sight and feeling.

Let us suppose two atmospheres, one above the other; the upper one let us call the region of faith, the lower one the region of sense. It is to be feared that many of God's children are walking more frequently in the lower atmos-

phere of sight and feeling than in the upper
one of faith. And so we see constantly, when
God removes those blessings and gifts which
are visible, all their joy goes ! Proving that
it was not the joy of *faith*, but the joy of *sense*,
they were living upon. But the believer's
true sphere is the upper one—he ought never
to forsake it—" for we walk by faith, *not
by sight.*" How clearly and beautifully St.
Peter puts it, "Whom having *not seen*, ye
love; in whom, though now *ye see Him not*,
yet *believing*, ye *rejoice*, with joy unspeakable
and full of glory" (1 Pet. i. 8). That is the
"joy of *faith*." Take, again, that passage
in Hab. iii. 17, 18, "Although the fig tree
shall not blossom, neither shall fruit be in
the vines; the labour of the olive shall fail,
and the fields shall yield no meat; the flock
shall be cut off from the fold, and there shall
be no herd in the stalls"—everything in the
things of sense calculated to cause sadness
and gloom—"Yet," says the prophet, "I will
rejoice." Unbelief would have said "'*there-*

fore' I am cast down—I cannot but be miserable." But faith says "YET I will"—not simply hope or trust, but—"*rejoice* in the Lord, I will *joy* in the God of my salvation." This is "the joy of *faith.*"

To rejoice on account of our attainments, or of our victories, is not "the joy of *faith.*"

We read of the Seventy how that they " returned again with joy, saying, Lord, even the devils are subject unto us through Thy name" (Luke x. 17). But this was not to be the ground of their joy. Triumph over Satan, through Christ's name, should fill us with gratitude; but in the very hour of victory there is a danger of secretly cherishing a boastful spirit. Self, in some subtle form, will seek to enter in. " Rejoice not," said our Lord, that the spirits are subject unto you; but rather rejoice because your names are written in heaven." He would not take away their joy—only He would have them rest it, not on the things of sight or of sense, but on the things of faith. It would then

be a joy that would be abiding and perma-
nent.

Take another illustration : Paul and Silas
in the prison at Philippi. What is their condition as regards the things of sense? The
most gloomy and miserable. They had been
roughly handled, cruelly beaten, thrust into
the inner prison, and their feet made fast in
the stocks. And at midnight, at the darkest
hour, what did they do? They "prayed and
sang praises." Here, then, was not only earnest desire but *joy*—and a joy that sprang not
from the things of sense but the things of
faith.

The secret of this joy lies in living upon
the facts revealed to faith—and not being so
influenced by the things of sense as to be
cast down when they are discouraging, and
elated when they are bright and prosperous.
" None of *these things* move me," may be
the true testimony of every child of God
who really walks by faith. The things that
do move him are those which are revealed

to his soul in the Scriptures by the Holy
Spirit.

If our joy is the "joy of *faith*," it will be
an even and abiding gladness of heart, because He who is the source and ground of it
is "*the same* yesterday, and to-day, and for
ever."

III.—THE "TRIAL OF FAITH."

There are various kinds of trial. There is
the trial of the sincerity of our love (2 Cor.
viii. 8), the trial of our work (1 Cor. iii. 13),
the trial of our hearts (1 Thess. ii. 4) ; but all
these are intimately connected with our *faith*.
"I have prayed for thee," said our Lord to
Peter, "that thy *faith* fail not" (Luke xxii.
32). It was a trial of his sincerity, of his
love, of his courage, but, more than all, of his
faith, and especially *after* he had fallen. So
the same Apostle writes (1 Pet. i. 7): "That
the trial of your *faith*, being much more
precious than of gold that perisheth, though

D

it be tried with fire, might be found unto praise, and honour, and glory, at the appearing of Jesus Christ.''

But are all trials, trials of our faith ? In the history of God's children, much of the suffering they have to pass through is the consequence of their own disobedience. Take, for instance, the greatest example of faith we have given us in the Word of God—the greatest human example—Abraham. We have, in his history, the most wonderful illustration of the trial of faith; but we have in that history also a very striking example of a child of God suffering on account of his own unfaithfulness. So that we must distinguish between those trials which are sent of God, to prove or test our faith, and those trials which are sent to chasten us for our sins.

We see Abraham, in the twenty-first chapter of Genesis, in deep sorrow. He was severely tried when the command came : "Cast out the bond-woman and her son; for the son of this bond-woman shall not be heir with my son, even with Isaac." That Abraham felt this trial we know, from the words, "And the thing was very grievous in Abraham's sight, because of his son." But all this bitter suffering Abraham might have been spared, had he not previously stepped out of the path of implicit obedience and simple trust. He was here enduring the chastening which the sin recorded in chap. xvi. had brought upon him, in hearkening to the voice of Sarah, instead of waiting only upon God for the fulfiment of the promise. Are not many of our trials of this character?

But there are other trials which are sent, not as chastisements for our sins, but as *tests* of our faith, for its exercise, its manifestation, and its strengthening. To this class of suffering belongs that which was unquestionably *the* greatest and most severe of all Abraham's trials. It comes to him towards the close of his life. God had fulfilled His promise, and had given him a son. All his hopes were

bound up in that son; for God had said: " I
will establish my covenant with him for an
everlasting covenant, and with his seed after
him" (chap. xvii. 19). He expected, therefore,
that that son would grow up and become the
father of many nations. And yet the Divine
command comes to him: " Take now thy son,
thine only son Isaac, whom thou lovest, and
get thee into the land of Moriah; and *offer
him there for a burnt-offering* upon one of the
mountains which I will tell thee of." Here
was a trial which was emphatically a trial of
faith. It was a test to prove whether he
could still continue to *believe* the Word which
Jehovah had spoken.

See the extreme difficulty of Abraham's
position. The Divine command seemed to
be in direct conflict with the Divine promise.
If he obeys the command, how could the
promise be fulfilled? If he holds fast to the
promise, how could the command be obeyed?
Here, then, was the trial of his faith. *He
must obey, and believe.* Do what God says,

and trust Him to fulfil what He had promised.
As to *how* God would keep His promise, he
had nothing to do. The trial lay in this—a
temptation *to doubt the possibility of the
promise being fulfilled* if the command were
obeyed.

We see that the trial of faith implies a
promise; the object of the trial being to prove
the *tenacity* with which we cling to that
promise, in spite of everything that tends to
shake our confidence. It may be that some
who read these pages are passing through
this very trial; it may be they are being
tempted, in a very special way, to doubt the
certainty of those "precious promises" which
God has given us pertaining to godliness.
As, for instance, that He is able to make *all
grace* abound toward us (2 Cor. ix. 8); able to
keep us from falling (Jude 24); able to save to
the uttermost (Heb. vii. 25); that He will
supply *all our need* (Phil. iv. 19); that He
will keep him in peace whose mind is stayed
on Him (Isa. xxvi. 3); that sin shall not have

dominion over us (Rom. vi. 14); that He is able to do exceeding abundantly above all that we ask or think (Eph. iii. 20).

How many a child of God continues weak and timid because, instead of being occupied with *what* God has promised, he is considering *how* it can be fulfilled. But, as we have seen, we have nothing to do with the *how;* it is enough that God has given us His Word. Whatever, therefore, may be the nature of the suffering or trial through which we have to pass, let us ever account that God is able to fulfil all His promises (Heb. xi. 19). Let nothing ever lead us to doubt the *certainty* of His Word, though we may be utterly at a loss to understand the *manner* in which He may see fit to accomplish it. We shall then be able to testify, with Joshua of old: "Not one thing hath failed of all the good things which the LORD your God spake concerning you; all are come to pass unto you, and not one thing hath failed thereof."

Divine Power.

THERE can be no doubt that the great need of the Church in the present day is more *power*. While there is much light and Gospel truth, there is comparatively but little spiritual power. To *know* the " exceeding greatness of God's power to usward who believe " must be the desire of every true child of God. We all have certain notions as to what this power is. But these notions may not be exactly Scriptural. We all think we know how this power is to be obtained. But here, it is possible, we may make serious mistakes. Let us consider, first,

WHAT IT IS.

It is not *excitement*. Perhaps there are some who are inclined to think that without great emotion there can be no power. But spiritual power may be unaccompanied by any great manifestation of feeling. It may exist without any outward emotion as a calm, irresistible influence.

Again, it is not *self-energy*. How many associate spiritual power with so much self-effort. So that great effort is regarded as a sure sign of great power. Instead of which it is just the reverse. A little child, by means of great effort, raises a weight which a full-grown man lifts with little or no effort. The struggles of the soul, though evidences of life, are not marks of strength, but signs of weakness.

Again, *Power does not mean self-sufficiency*. It does not imply that God has made *us* all-sufficient; that *we* are strong, that we are now able as of ourselves to overcome. This would be to produce confidence in self— instead of confidence in God.

1. Let us fully recognise the fact that it is GOD's *power*. It is *always* His power. Even when it is being put forth *in* us, it is God's power. It is not something we get *from* Him

to be exercised *by us*. This would be to make us independent of Him. But we are never so really dependent on Him as when we are fully under the influence of His power. It is then that He works in us " both to will and to do of His good pleasure." We are then the willing instruments in His hand. We read in Acts xix. 11: "*God* wrought special miracles by the hands of Paul." Some would have said "Paul wrought special miracles by means of God." But it was God by Paul—not Paul by God. God was the worker—Paul was only the instrument. So the Apostle said of himself, " I also labour, striving according to His working, which *worketh in me mightily* " (Col. i. 29). The recognition of this fact, then, that it is not our own, but God's power, will take away from us all ground of boasting, all occasion for pride. We are never more conscious of its being God's power than when we are really being carried along by its influence.

2. *It is the Power of Christ's Resurrection.*

The power of His *life*. His *risen* life. There
was a mighty power in His death. It secured
for us a full deliverance. But this is the virtue
or power of His life—of an endless life;
which has nothing before it—no judgment,
no death, no cloud. "Christ the *power* of
God." Having been reconciled by His death
we are saved *in* His life" (Rom. v. 10). It
is there we are preserved, garrisoned as in a
fortress. Kept *in* the power of God" (1 Pet.
i. 5). It is to know more of Him as *the* life,
out of death, that the believer prays—" That
I may know Him and the *power* of His resurrection" (Phil. iii. 10).

3. *It is the Power of the Holy Ghost.* The
Holy Ghost is the Spirit of power. "We
have not received the Spirit of fear, but of
power, and of love, and of a sound mind."
To be filled with the Spirit is to be endued
with power. To walk in the Spirit is to live
in the power of God, and to be kept from
being overcome by the power of sin.

HOW IS THIS POWER MANIFESTED ?

Not merely in good desires, but in practical
results. It is a blessed thing to desire the
good; but there is something more blessed
still, and that is doing the good. There are
many who get as far as good aims and sincere
longings after holiness, but how to *perform*
that which is good they find not. If the
Gospel brought us simply to this point,—to
know God's will, to desire to do it, but to remain utterly unable to walk in it, then we
should be of "all men the most miserable."
But, while we have no sufficiency in ourselves, we have all-sufficiency in God. "I can
do all things in Christ." *There* is the provision
for our obedience—and it is a *full* provision.

1. Divine Power manifests itself in *Faith
towards God*. A man's spiritual strength will
be in proportion to his faith. A strong man
is a man of strong faith. But what does that
mean ? Simply this. Perfect human *weakness
resting on Divine Omnipotence*. There was a
poor woman in Scotland very well known for

her wonderful faith. Some one who went to
see her said, " Are you the woman of great
faith ?" " No," she said, " I am the woman
of weak faith in a *great God*." The strength
is not in the faith that trusts, but in the
Person in whom we trust. That which brings
our weakness to rest wholly on Divine
strength, is faith—and then it is that God's
power fills us and is put forth through us.
Abraham was a man " Strong in faith." It
was through faith that the Old Testament
worthies " Subdued kingdoms, wrought righteousness, obtained promises, stopped the
mouths of lions, quenched the violence of fire,
escaped the edge of the sword, out of weakness were made strong, waxed valiant in
fight, turned to flight the armies of the aliens "
(Heb. xi. 33, 34).

2. Divine Power manifests itself in *love to
our fellow-men*. It shows itself not only in what
it can do, but in what it can bear. " Beareth
all things—endureth all things." It strengthens us " unto all patience." Here then is a test

of Spiritual strength—not How much do you know? or How much can you teach?—but How much can you endure for Christ's sake? Are you meek under rebuke—are you patient when you are misunderstood, misrepresented, or falsely accused? Our answer to this may show us how much we need " to be strengthened with might by His Spirit in the inner man."

3. Again, it manifests itself in *our own peace of mind and self-control.* We say *self*-control, and yet it is not self after all that controls, but God. It is in fact self surrendered to God. It is God's peace keeping the heart and mind. Here is an evidence of power—a calm subdued tone of mind, a mind kept well in hand, in God's hand. Not easily ruffled, not soon carried away by praise, nor cast down and discouraged by censure; but a mind well balanced, calm and restful. Such was the Apostle's mind who could say, in the prospect of the severest trials, " None of these things move me." Divine power is that which gives depth, solidity and steadiness to the soul.

HOW TO BE IN GOD'S POWER.

We say how to be *in* it, rather than how to *get* it, because it is not a thing to be carried away, to be used and possessed apart from God. It is that which is to carry us—to use us. The reason why we do not enjoy this blessing in greater measure is to be found in certain hindrances that must be got rid of.

1. *Cease from self.*—How infinite are the forms in which self appears. Some are occupied with good self. They pride themselves on their excellencies. Others are just as much occupied with *bad* self. They are for ever groaning over their imperfections, and struggling with the flesh as if they hoped in time to improve it. When shall we be convinced it is so utterly bad that it is beyond all recovery? Our experience, upward, in the power of God, is just in proportion to our experience, downward, in ceasing from self.

Is it, Reckon yourself to be *weak* in reference to sin? No, it is lower than that. Is it, Reckon yourself to be *dying?* No, lower still. "Reckon yourself to be *dead*—(Rom. vi. 6,)—indeed unto sin." Some believe they are very weak. But what does that imply? That they have *some* strength. But when a man is *dead* he has *no* strength. We must act on the assumption that we are dead in reference to sin.

We shall not then speak of difficulty as to resisting temptation in reference to ourselves. We shall take the lowest place, and say it is impossible. But we shall know that what is impossible with self is possible with God. We shall take our place on the resurrection-side of the Cross, and in so doing we leave behind the old self-life which was crucified with Christ. The Cross thus divides the old self-life from the new Christ-life. To live in Him who is the Life, is to be in the power of God.

2. *Yield yourself wholly to God.*

We know what yielding to *sin* means. By so doing we have been brought under its power. Now yield to *God*, and you will know His power.

We have not to make it or to increase it, but to submit to be carried by it. For it is like a mighty tide that flows on with calm but irresistible force. Imagine yourself in a little boat on some broad but rapid river. The current flows on, but you remain in the same place. I ask you, "How is it you make no progress?" You say you cannot tell. You make great efforts by rowing hard to move along, but without success. At last I discover the cause—you are moored to the shore. What you want is not more effort—more struggles at the oars—but being set free from the land. You need to let go your hold of the shore, and to yield yourself to the stream; to abandon yourself to the tide of His conquering power. There may be more than one anchor that needs to be pulled up. But every hindrance must be removed; every rope must be cut before you can know in your own experience the "power of His resurrection."

3. *Trust Him to supply all your need.*

A soul wholly yielded is a soul that finds no difficulty in believing. The hindrance to faith is the want of surrender. That hindrance being removed, trust is no longer impossible. To trust is to rest, and to rest is not to carry—but to consent to be carried. It is as we rest in the Lord that we partake of His power. "In returning and rest shall ye be saved; in quietness and in confidence shall be your strength" (Isa. xxx. 15).

"Dead unto Sin."

THE trouble of the believer who knows Christ as his justification is not sin as to its *guilt*, but sin as to its ruling *power*. In other words, it is not from sin as a load, or an offence, that he seeks to be freed—for he sees that God has completely acquitted him from the charge and penalty of sin—but it is from sin as a *master*. To know God's way of deliverance from sin as a master he must apprehend the truth contained in the sixth chapter of Romans. There we see what God has done, not with our *sins*—that question the Apostle has dealt with in the preceding chapters — but with *ourselves*, the agents and slaves of sin. He has put our old man—our original self—where He put our sins, namely, on the cross with Christ. " Knowing this, that our old man was crucified with Christ " (Rom. vi. 6). The believer there sees not only that Christ died *for* him —substitution—but that he died *with* Christ —identification. And that death is regarded as a past event — a thing accomplished. "How shall we that *died*" (not that *are dead*, as in our English version) "to sin live any longer therein?" The particular time and event referred to is the death of Christ on the cross. This, then, is not an attainment true only of some of God's children; it is a fact affirmed of *all* believers alike, whether they realise it or not.

But we must see the *design* of that death— of our identification with Christ in His death —if we would know experimentally the sanctifying effects secured to us thereby.

To Christ's death *for* me, God has joined, as a consequence, the complete justification of my soul from the charge of sin. The *fact* that He *did* die for me, I *accept* as a reality; the *purpose*, that I should be accounted righteous as the consequence of that fact, I *reckon* as a present, imputed blessing. So in regard to sin's dominion.

God's purpose in identifying me with Christ in His death was that I should be legally released from my old master, Sin, so that I should no longer serve him. The *fact* that I was crucified with Christ I *accept* as a reality; the *purpose* that I should henceforth account myself dead to sin's claims, I *reckon* as my present privilege and duty. And this is the very substance of the exhortation in the eleventh verse, " Likewise reckon ye also yourselves to be dead indeed unto sin," &c.

But it has been objected that the force of the word " likewise" is against such an interpretation. " Reckon yourselves *likewise* "— that is, *like as* Christ *died* unto sin. So are you to reckon yourselves, &c.

Now, *How did Christ die unto sin?* it is asked. Christ did not die to the *dominion* of it, or the *service* of it. Hence, it is argued, it is not in this sense we are to reckon ourselves to be dead to it. But He died to the *guilt*

and charge of it.   So it is in that sense, and
in that sense alone, we must understand the
exhortation, " Reckon ye yourselves to be
dead unto sin."   Reckon yourselves, and not
Christ only, as dead unto the charge of sin ;
and as you realise that God has forgive you,
and will not impute sin to you, so you will
find that the power of sin is broken in your
daily life.   This is the argument often used
against the foregoing interpretation.   And in
this way the passages in this chapter manifestly bearing on our *walk*, that is our sanctification, are taken simply in connection with
our justification.

But we submit that by such a view of the
passage we entirely miss the Apostle's meaning, and fail to appropriate the blessed and
glorious benefits it is intended to convey.-

Take an illustration.   Imagine yourself a
slave.   You have been bought by a new
master, you enter into that master's service ;
you are his property.   Suppose the old master
comes and asks you to perform some work

for him. If you recognised your true position how would you act ? Surely you would
act consistently with the fact that you had
been purchased by the new master, and you
would reckon yourself released from the service of the old one. In other words, you
would reckon yourself to be dead *in relation*
to your old master. And just in proportion
as you *thus* treated him, would he find you
like a corpse (νεκροὺς—Rom. vi. 11), impas-
sive and immovable, in relation to his solici-
tations.

So in like manner—when Sin, our old
master, tempts us, and entices us to engage
in his service, this is the way God would
have us treat him. Seeing that it is a *fact*
that we *have died* with Christ unto sin on the
cross, and thus become *legally* released from
sin's claims, we are now to *reckon* ourselves
actually free, or *to be dead indeed unto him.*
Treat him as if you were absolutely dead.
Neither he nor you are so really—but treat him
as if *you* were dead. It is not, treat him as

if *he* were dead. Sin is not dead, nor are we commanded to reckon it as dead. But we are to reckon ourselves dead *in relation to it*.

The slave who passes into the possession of a new master is legally free from the service of his old master. That old master, let us suppose, is still alive—he is not dead. Nor is the slave really a corpse—but knowing that the old master has no longer any authority over him, the slave is dead in *relation to him*. Only in relation to him is he dead. If he were a corpse he would be dead to everything in the world. But he reckons himself dead only in reference to the claims of his old master. Just so, you who have died with Christ—you are not dead absolutely —but in *relation* to your old master, Sin, it is your duty and privilege thus to reckon yourself. It is not ye *may* not but " ye *cannot* serve two masters."

Let us understand the true meaning of the word " Reckon." It has been said: "We do not ask a person to reckon anything to be what it manifestly is. No one would say of five sovereigns, 'Reckon that to be five pounds,' for it *is* that; but such language may be appropriately used of a bank-note or a cheque, or of anything which represents that amount."

So, if the *purpose* of our identification with Christ in His death (which was that we should be released from sin's service) were a matter of consciousness, it would no longer be a matter for reckoning. And yet, *as* we reckon, *so* we *experience*, a deliverance from sin's dominion. The reckoning of faith is the way to the consciousness of experience.

It is in the sixth verse of this chapter that we have this purpose stated : " Knowing that our old man was crucified with Him " (the fact) "that the body of sin might be destroyed, that henceforth we should not serve sin " (the purpose). Let us first understand what is meant by "*the body of sin.*" Dr. Vaughan remarks :—" *The body of (belonging to) sin.*

Not a mere periphasis of *sin*, as if it were
the *substance* or *sum of sin;* but rather to be
understood (as the context shows) of *the
material body in its present unregenerate state,
as the inlet of temptation and the agent of
sin*." Dean Alford also remarks we are not
to understand it as meaning "*the totality
of sin; nor the substance or essence of sin,*
nor the *mass of sin;* but the *body which
belongs to,* or *serves sin,* in which sin rules or
is manifest." Wordsworth renders it: "The
body of sin" *is our body so far as it is the
seat and instrument of sin, and the slave of
sin*."

The purpose, then, of that death with Christ
was that this body, hitherto the slave of sin,
might be *delivered* from sin's authority,—or
might be "reduced to a state of inaction
and impotence" (*Dr. Vaughan*)—so that we
should no longer serve sin. (See note at the
end of this chapter.)

The *fact* we are to *accept* as a past reality.
The *purpose* we are to *reckon* as our present

condition in reference to sin. We died with
Christ that we *should be*—having died let
us now *reckon* that we *are*—dead indeed unto
sin.

By the Act of Emancipation Abraham
Lincoln set free *legally,* in order to set free
practically, every slave. Before, however,
this could be actually realised each slave
must hear the good news. Then, accepting
the *fact* that the Act had been passed—had
become law—each one had now to *reckon* the
purpose of that Act as really accomplished,
and refuse any longer to be a slave; and by
so doing the *reckoning* of faith was imme-
diately followed by the reality of experience;
provided, of course, that the slave had power
to enforce his right of freedom.

So let us treat our old master, Sin. We
have nothing now to do with him. He has
no more claim upon us; and if we treat him
as God bids us do we shall find he has no
power to compel us to serve Him. When he
entices you to sin let him meet with the

same response from you as he would from
one actually dead.   Reckon that the *purpose*
of your dying with Christ is a present reality,
and, as you thus reckon, faith will pass into
experience.   And so " sin shall not lord it
over you."

NOTE.—The word (καταργέω) which, in Rom. vi. 11,
is rendered " destroyed " occurs twenty-seven times in
the New Testament.   " The English Version gives it
no less than seventeen various renderings in the twenty-
seven places of its occurrence." (*Vaughan.*)   In Rom.
vii. it occurs twice (vv. 2 and 6) rendered " loosed " and
" delivered."   In the other places it is translated " to
make without effect," " make void," " bring to
nought," &c.

"Alive unto God."

ONE difficulty experienced by many in connection with the Sixth Chapter of Romans has been expressed in the following words :—" I do not understand what is meant by reckoning myself *dead* unto sin—I have tried to obey the command ; but I do not *feel* that I am dead to sin. *I do not realise this deadness.*"

Let us first clearly understand that the Apostle does not say that the " new nature " is to reckon the " old nature " dead. The truth is, in this chapter the Apostle is not discussing the question of the two natures at all. He here regards the believer simply as one. The " old man " in the sixth verse must not be understood as referring to a *part* of his former self—the flesh. He himself, the believer in his unrenewed state, with no other nature in him but the flesh, was the "old man." It is our old self—"our former self, personality before our new birth," as Dean Alford interprets it. This old or former self was crucified with Christ. They were to recollect this fact—"knowing this"—verse 6. But as Christ was now *alive* from the dead, they were to reckon themselves also as alive unto God in Him. It is in this Christ-life, which is a life unto God, that they are dead unto sin. The eleventh verse does not express *a two-fold state* (one nature dead unto sin, and the other nature alive unto God), but a spiritual position or sphere (to be maintained by faith), having a *twofold relation*—unto sin, dead —unto God, alive.

Let us consider what that position is. It is *life in Christ*—a life *out* of death. This death was not only *for* sin as an offence—in which sense Christ died *alone*—but a death *unto* sin as a *person*—in which sense we died *with Him*.

Sin is in this chapter *personified*. He has a kingdom (chap. v. 21 verse). He has slaves (vi. 17, 20). He demands obedience (ver. 16).

He seeks to have dominion (12, 14). He asserts His authority over, and seeks to usurp possession of, our mortal bodies (ver. 12). He pays wages to those who serve Him (ver. 23).

When Christ came into the world He encountered Sin as a person. He was daily exposed to sin's assaults. He continually suffered from sin's opposition. But though sin continually brought his *power* against Christ, he never succeeded in exercising *lordship* over Him. That "Holy One" never yielded to sin's temptations, never obeyed his demands.

Now it was at the *cross* Christ died *unto* sin considered as a person, once and for ever. "In that He died He died unto sin once."

The *cross* thus becomes to the believer, who is identified with Christ in His death, the point of separation from sin. He may come to you with all his tempting power, but if you meet him as *dead on the cross with Christ*, he will have no dominion over you.

In relation to sin you must reckon that as

your condition, but in relation to God you are
" Alive *in* Jesus Christ our Lord." It is our
privilege, nay, it is our duty, thus to reckon
ourselves—and by faith to occupy that position.

We may take that position by faith the
moment we know Christ as our Saviour.
And, whilst there, sin can come to us only as
a *person*—not as a *master*. It is when we fail
to maintain faith's reckoning (as in verse 11)
that sin, which first tempted us, now overcomes us. He is then our *master*.

To meet sin as a *master* is to endeavour *to
make ourselves free*. But this is to take a lower
ground than that which belongs to us in our
Risen Christ. " Stand fast in the liberty
wherewith Christ *hath* made us free." The
Apostle assumes that you have taken that
position of freedom to start with; which is,
to be no longer in the relation of a slave to
sin, but to be delivered from his service.
When he comes to you, therefore, it is as a
person, with the view of course of becoming

again your master. Now the question is,
"How are we to meet him?" "Reckon
yourselves dead unto him." The moment
that you begin to fight with him, that moment
you cease to be dead to him—no matter how
resolutely you may struggle against him—
and the moment you cease to treat him as if
you were a corpse, that moment you begin to
know him as your master. For it is then
that we forsake our true position, which is
one of freedom from sin as a master. Let it
be remembered we are to fight "the good
fight of *faith*," which consists in *maintaining* a
position of freedom - and not in *obtaining* that
position. We are to fight not *for* it, but *from*
it. He alone has obtained it. It is God's
free gift. The gift of God is eternal life *in*
Jesus Christ our Lord (ver. 23). Christ first
of all places us there. Let us be fully abiding
in that life, and Sin, when he comes, will find
us dead unto him.

Our great aim then should be to maintain
faith's position, to abide in that sphere, in

which sin does not become to us more than
a person who seeks to be a master—and that
position is the Christ-life.   May we experimentally know more of this.   May we more
continually view our privileges from this side
of truth !   "Alive unto God in Jesus Christ
our Lord."

" Buried with Christ," and raised with Him too ;
   What is there left for me to do ?
   Simply to cease from struggling and strife,
   Simply to "walk in newness of life."
      Glory be to God.
                                        RYDER.

Danger Signals.

"If we say we have no sin, we deceive ourselves, and the truth is not in us."—1 *John* i. 8.

HOW often is this text quoted by the nominal Christian, as if it were an excuse for continuing in sin. And sometimes we have heard it referred to as an argument against the possibility of being freed in this life from the service of sin.

But if there are those who thus abuse this passage of Scripture, let us by no means fall into the opposite delusion by concluding, as some have done, that the text does not refer to the believer at all.

Nothing is clearer, as we see from the context, than that the persons addressed are the true children of God, and that the danger against which we are warned is that which meets us at the point of highest privilege.

It is not a temptation to which a careless
worldling, or even an inconsistent believer,
is exposed. As Dr. Candlish says : " It is
not deliberate hypocrisy that we are here
warned against; but a far more subtle form
of falsehood, and one apt *more easily to beset us,
as believers,* even when most seriously and
earnestly bent on " walking in the light as
God is in the light." The danger " lies in
the line of our sanctification." " For a time
the new insight we have got, under that light
in which we walk, into the spiritual law of
God, and into our own carnal selves, keeps us
shut up into Christ; and into that continual
sprinkling of His blood upon us, without
which we cannot have a moment's peace, or
a moment's sense of being cleansed from sin.
But gradually we come to be more at ease.
We cannot be altogether insensible to the
growing satisfaction of our new standing with
God, and our new feelings towards Him.
Before the fervour of our first fresh love, inward struggles are hushed. The evil that but

yesterday seemed so unconquerable ceases to
make itself so acutely felt. The crisis is
past; the war, as a war to the knife, is ended;
grace prevails; iniquity, as ashamed, hides
its face.

"Ah! then begins the secret lurking inclination to cherish within myself some
thought equivalent to 'saying that I have
no sin.' It may not so express itself. It
may not be self-acknowledged, or even self-
conscious. It comes insidiously as a thief
to steal away my integrity before I am
aware of it. Remaining corruption in me
ceases gradually to give trouble or dis-
tress. A certain lethargic proneness to ac-
quiesce in things as they are creeps over
me. I am not conscious of anything very
far amiss in my spiritual experience or in
my practical behaviour. I begin to 'say
that I have no sin.'

"But 'I deceive myself, and the truth is
not in me.' I am fast sinking into my old
natural habit of evasion and equivocation,

of self-excuse and self-justification. ' Guile' is taking the place of ' truth '—the truth of God —' in my spirit,' ' in my inward parts.' I cease to be as sensitively alive as I once was to whatever in me or about me cannot stand the light. I am thus incurring a serious hazard: the hazard of being found ' walking in darkness,' and so disqualifying myself for fellowship with ' Him who is light.' And I am apt to lose a very precious privilege : the privilege of continual and constant confession, in order to continual and constant forgiveness." We believe this witness is true.

Let us thank God, then, for so lovingly giving us this safeguard against such a danger.

The use of such passages of Scripture may be made clearer by an illustration.

We all like to travel by express train. But speed alone is not all that is essential. Suppose as you are entering the carriage the guard comes up and informs you that the

"express," by which you are about to travel,
will be run that day without "brakes," or
"danger signals." However great might be
your desire to have plenty of steam, no consideration would induce you to risk your life
on such a wild and reckless journey.

So God, in His word, has not only instructed us concerning the mighty power by
which the believer is to be filled, but He has
also graciously given us certain safeguards to
preserve us from running off the lines of
"truth and soberness."

Let no man, therefore, presume, under any
plea whatever, to remove the danger-signals
which God Himself has placed on the line of
the believer's sanctification. Let us take these
words, and similar passages of Scripture, as
they stand, and accept them in their plain
and evident meaning. And while we would
zealously testify to the unlimited power and
fulness we have in Christ for " cleansing from
all unrighteousness," as well as for the pardon
of all sin, let us never suppose we can ever

attain an experience or arrive at a condition in this life, in which we may say truthfully " we have no sin " ; or, what is equivalent to it, that we no longer need continually the power and efficacy of the cleansing blood.

Obedience.

ARE there not many of God's children who seem to be afraid of looking at the obeying side of the Christian life? The very word *obedience* suggests to them the thought of bondage and legality. And yet nothing is clearer than that obedience is one of the highest privileges of the Gospel dispensation. The law shows us that it is a *right* thing, but it is only "in Christ" we find it to be a *joyous* thing to obey, because it is only in Him we find the *power* for obedience.

The question is not, Does God expect of me a life of "good works"? No enlightened soul can doubt for a moment the importance and necessity of the "fruits of righteousness," of practical obedience, in the daily walk. But the question is, *How* is this obedience to become possible?—*how* may conformity to the will of God become a free and joyous reality?

There are many sincere souls—earnest believers in Christ, who are seeking the true answer to this all-important question. To quote the words of a well-known, and much honoured Evangelical teacher:—" There are other labourers besides those who are seeking for pardon—for justification before God. There are labourers *after sanctification*—after personal holiness—after riddance of the power of the old Adam; and to such, as well as to those who are seeking after salvation, Christ gives this great invitation; to such He promises, with this great " I will " (Matt. xi. 28-30). It is highly possible for a man, after having found justifying rest in Christ, to enter upon a state of deep need as regards sanctifying rest. We think we shall not go far wrong if we say that this has been the experience of almost every believer that has ever lived." *

---

* Rev. Philip Bennet Power.—" *The I Wills of Christ*," *p.* 20.

There are many who have good desires; who thoroughly hate the evil under which they so continually fall, and who love the good they are striving to attain. But how to *perform* the good that they would they find not. That they are converted souls is clear, for they *delight* in the law of God after the inward man. Now, it is to such we would very earnestly say, Come to the written word of God. Let no man hinder you from a candid and prayerful consideration of the subject. Ask yourself, Does my Heavenly Father set before me a path of obedience along which the Spirit and power of Christ *cannot* lead me? Is the provision made for me in Christ for practical holiness, *in*sufficient to meet the power of indwelling sin? These are vital questions. Let us not shrink from answering them by the word of God itself. If there is a better life—a truer, freer and holier life for you, than you have yet known, let no consideration keep you from its actual realisation. Tremendous responsibility rests upon those who by their influence and writings are discouraging you from seeking it. But remember you are no more justified in making this an excuse, than the Children of Israel were justified in saying, "Our brethren have discouraged our heart" (Deut. i. 28), as a plea for their disobedience and unbelief.

If we ask What is the character of that life for which we have been redeemed at such an infinite cost? let the Scriptures give the answer. St. Paul tells us we are "created in Christ Jesus *unto good works*, which God hath before ordained"(prepared) "that we should *walk in them*" (Eph. ii. 10). St. Peter tells us we are "Elect according to the foreknowledge of God the Father, through sanctification of the Spirit *unto obedience*," &c. (1 Pet. i. 2). St. John tells us, "This is the love of God, that we *keep His commandments:* and His commandments are *not grievous*" (1 John v. 3).

Here, then, we see the Divine *purpose* of

our regeneration. The same inspired Word that reveals to us the Divine *will* as the *path* of obedience, declares also that there is for us the Divine *power* as the *means* of obedience. Let us not separate these two. things.

Now the essence of all true obedience is the submission of the will to God. It is more than good words—or sound views—or devout feelings—or even right actions. It is the surrender of the whole heart to God, and an implicit dependence upon Him for all that He has promised. Not one act once for all— but an attitude maintained day by day. The outcome of this heart-submission, and simple trust in Him, will be the spontaneous conformity of the life in good works, through the power of the Holy Ghost.

It is remarkable that the Apostle uses the same word in Phil. ii. 12, "*work out your* own salvation"; and in Eph. vi. 13, "*having done* all to stand," that he uses in Rom. vii. 18, "but how to *perform* that which is good I find not." Things not possible of accomplishment *from* himself—even as a converted and renewed soul—were possible *in* and *from* Christ. " Our sufficiency is of (*from*) God " (2 Cor. iii. 5). " I can do all things *in Christ* which strengtheneth me " (Phil. iv. 13).

The Believer's Provision.

IN the well-known saying of St. Augustine, "Give what Thou commandest, and then command what Thou wilt," we have not only the pith of the Gospel for the sinner who needs pardon, but the substance of the truth for the believer seeking holiness. If we would receive God's commands, without being brought into legal bondage, we must know God's gift, without limiting it, in its fulness, or freeness, or present efficacy. *God's requirement* of us His children—forgiven, justified, and set apart in Christ—should not be contemplated apart from *God's provision* for us, who, in ourselves, are utterly insufficient. It is as we see that "our sufficiency is of *God*"— that is, not only *of* Him as the first cause, but *from* Him as the immediate source—that we find by experience that "His commandments are not grievous."

It is true that all God requires of us we
lack; but it is also true that all we need He
supplies. The believer can give thanks that
God has supplied all his need as to standing;
the same God engages to supply all his need
as to walk. But while we see God's requirement, and recognise God's provision, let us
not overlook *our responsibility*. When we fail,
it is to this our failure may be traced. It is
not because the provision has been insufficient,
or unavailable, or afar off—but because the
channel has been obstructed, the avenues of
the soul have been closed, so that the need
has remained unsupplied. Our responsibility
lies in the exercise of faith.

Because it is impossible to exaggerate the
all-sufficiency and never-failing efficacy of the
provision which God has made for His children, in Christ, for their sanctification, we may
step out upon every duty, however difficult,
without anxiety; we can *rest* in His name, in
every trial, without fear; we can *receive* all
His dispensations, however mysterious, with-

out doubt or murmuring; and we can *yield* up ourselves and all our members to Him, without reserve. Faith in all these aspects must be brought into exercise—and here is our responsibility. There must be the courage of faith, the rest of faith, the receptivity of faith, and the surrender of faith. It is then that *our need* becomes linked to *God's provision*.

How precious is the promise, " My God shall supply all your need according to His riches in glory by Christ Jesus " (Phil. iv. 19). " *My* God "—the Apostle's God, what he realised Him to be. " Shall *supply* "—shall *fill to the full*. " *All* your need "—temporal or spiritual, present or future. " Your *need* "— not always the same thing as your desires, your cravings, but what *God* says you need : *He* knows your real wants. And mark the *measure* of the supply : " *According to* the riches of His glory "—not " out of," that would have been blessed, but " according to," that is, in proportion to His riches. Well may

the Apostle say, " He is able to do exceeding
abundantly *above all that we ask or think*."

Then observe how God supplies our need !
What is the supply ?   " By Christ Jesus "—
or, literally, " IN Christ Jesus." A man perish-
ing from hunger has his need supplied through
the kindness of a friend.   The poor man's
supply is *in the food*, and not in the means
that brought it to him.   So Christ is not
the channel merely through which all God's
mercies descend to us, and by which all our
prayers ascend to Him—HE *is the supply itself*.
In this way God fills to the full all our need,
by unfolding by the Spirit some fresh fulness
of Christ, some further aspect of His un-
searchable riches.   But it is not so much by
something from Christ, as by Christ Himself
that He supplies all the needs of our souls.
How much is comprehended in that one word
" HIMSELF," when spiritually apprehended !
"Jesus shewed *Himself* to His disciples."

> " Thou, O Christ ! art all I want ;
> More than all in Thee I find."

G

Righteousness and Holiness.

THAT the Church has been aroused—if it has not yet been thoroughly awakened —to see not only the necessity, but the *possibility*, of a truer life, is a fact that none can deny. And that such an awakening should be accompanied by differences of opinion, is only what the experience of former ages in all similar revivals would lead us to expect. Collision and opposition are among the first evidences of a quickened Church, the characteristics of the earlier stages of returning life; to be followed by a deeper, fuller, and more vigorous vitality, in which bitterness, intolerance and discord shall give way to love, forbearance and harmony. We believe brighter days are near at hand, and that what we have hitherto seen is but the preparation for the realisation of spiritual blessings, such as

the Church has not known since the days of
the Apostles.

But " times of refreshing" are also times of
danger.   One thing we know—the truth has
nothing to lose, but everything to gain, by
thorough investigation and the most searching
inquiry.   But it is especially at such times
we need to be reminded that the " weapons
of our warfare are not carnal," and that " the
servant of the Lord must not strive " (wrangle),
"but be gentle unto all men, apt to teach,
patient, in meekness instructing those that
oppose themselves."

Again, in our zeal to bring out prominently
one particular truth, we may lead some to
conclude that we set very little value on
other truths equally necessary and important.
Nothing is more essential, for instance, to all
sound teaching, than that we build on the
right foundation ; and that we adhere closely
to the *divine order* in which truth is set forth
in the Word of God. Happily we live in a
day when Christians are not satisfied with

only the first principles of the doctrine of
Christ. Many are trying to help on and en-
courage all those who have apprehended
Christ as their Righteousness to know Him
more perfectly as their Sanctification.

But we would have our readers never to
forget that our first grand need as sinners is
not meetness for heaven—holiness, but a
judicial title to it — righteousness. There
must first be a just ground, a righteous
standing, for the sinner to occupy, before
there can be purity of heart or holiness of
life. In the "new creation" these two things
are essentially connected. They are not to
be confounded, nor are they to be separated.
The new man has, after God, been "created
in righteousness and holiness of truth" (Eph.
iv. 24). Righteousness is to holiness what
the foundation is to the superstructure. We
may be spending our time exclusively on the
foundation, by preaching nothing but justification by faith. And we may begin to build
the superstructure before the foundation has

been laid, by assuming that all are ready to
be instructed in holiness. The enemy in the
one case hinders the work already begun, in
the other he seeks to prevent its commence-
ment. But let us "not be ignorant of his
devices." Clearly, distinctly, and continually,
let us apprehend for ourselves, and let us
declare for the benefit of others, that Christ
alone, in His death and righteousness, is the
ground of our acceptance, and that by His
work *for* us, and not by His work *in* us, we
are justified and saved. "Other foundation
can no man lay than that is laid, which is
Jesus Christ." But let us not stop here.

As clearly, distinctly, and constantly, let
us bear in mind for ourselves, and make
known to all who have thus far apprehended
the truth, that Christ Himself—and not merely
a work in us which is the effect and not the
cause—Christ as a real, present and abiding
Saviour, is our Sanctification—the sanctuary
of our souls, our Life, in whom we abide and
by whom we are possessed. That it is in

this mutual indwelling by His Spirit that our purity and power consists; and that having Him, in whom it has pleased the Father that all fulness should dwell, we may do all things in Him who strengtheneth us, and abound to every good work.

The All-sufficiency of Christ.

IN a letter of Hewitson's, there occurs a sentence which is well worthy of repetition. He writes : — " Longinus says of Homer that he makes his gods mere men : *we may say of our unbelief that it makes the saving strength of Jehovah our Saviour less than the rebelling strength of our indwelling sin.*" To this source—low views of Christ's sufficiency—we may trace the cause of all our failures. While we have believed in Him as able to meet all our need in the matter of pardon and justification, we have failed to trust Him with the same implicit and simple confidence for deliverance from the bondage and service of sin. The power of sin against us we have secretly regarded as greater than the power of Christ for us, and yet could anything be more dishonouring to God than

such low and unbelieving thoughts of that
Son whom He has sent to be the *Saviour*
from all iniquity?   Not of the unsaved only,
but of the reconciled and forgiven, He seems
to ask that all-important question—"What
think ye of Christ?"   What do you think of
Him in reference to your *sanctification* as
well as your justification;   in reference to
your daily trials, your temptations, and conflicts with sin?   Is He as able to deliver you
from the *dominion* of all these as He is to
save you from the guilt and penalty of sin?
Is He an ALL-SUFFICIENT Saviour?   Get but
a view of His infinite power and of His
wondrous love—of His ability and willingness
to save, always and *now*,—and though your
foes may not become less, either in strength
or in number, you will rise to another sphere
of life, *above* the mists and fogs of unbelief
which have so long and so frequently shut out
the light of God's countenance from your soul.
You will rise to a position of deliverance
already obtained by Christ for you.

The joy and confidence of a child of God who is walking by faith, does not arise from any consciousness that the root of sin is eradicated, but from a sweet and hallowed assurance, founded on the word of God, of Christ's all-sufficiency in keeping it under, in breaking its power, and filling the soul with His own blessed Spirit, and in living His own life in us. The believer is not occupied with himself, but with Christ. It is not what *I* am or have become, but what *He is*, and is able to do, for and in me, that fills me with courage, and faith, and hope. " Moses wist not that the skin of His face shone." And yet he gave a testimony that it *did* shine, not by actually *speaking* about it, but by *shining*.

Let us not suppose, however, that no testimony to holiness is to be given by the lips. Though Christ and not self must be the subject of our testimony, yet we must tell out what *we are finding Christ can do for us* day by day. All God's children believe Christ is *able* to deliver them from their be-

setting sins.   But we want the testimony
that He *does* deliver them, that He *is leading*
them along a path which is "righteousness,
peace, and joy in the Holy Ghost." It is
salvation in its present-tense aspect that
we so greatly need to be prominently and
definitely presented to those who have
thoroughly grasped salvation in its past and
finished sense.   It is a constant view of
Him "who delivered us," and who "doth
deliver," and who "will yet deliver us," that
we need, to keep us from being overcome by
the temptations of sin and unbelief.

———

"The faith which enables the soul to abide
in Christ is nothing else than an assured trust
and confidence on our part that, as He has
already wrought out FOR us our acceptance
with God, so He will work IN us every gracious
disposition (be it repentance, or faith itself, or
humility, or hope, or love) which is necessary
to qualify us for glory.   It is not enough to

supplicate these graces; we must lean upon
Him for them, and fix the eye of expectation
upon the promise of His new Covenant: " I
will put my laws into their mind, and write
them in their hearts :" being well assured
that He will fulfil to us the terms thereof.
There is a promise, I say, that He will fulfil in
us all the work of sanctification ; and it is well
that it is so, by way of making assurance
doubly sure, and giving to the doubtful heart a
strong consolation. . . . . If the soul has the
least scintillation of a desire to be holy ; much
more if it is bent on being holy, as far as its
power goes; still more if it is striving and
struggling to be holy, and beating against the
cage of its corruptions in a great longing for
spiritual freedom, as a poor imprisoned bird
beats, who sees outside the bright sun and the
green trees, and other birds flitting to and fro
in the blue ether,—is it conceivable that the
Incarnate love, the love which bled, and
agonised, and poured itself out in death for
the objects on which it had fastened, should

not meet that desire, that longing, that striving, and visit the soul with power? As without holiness no man shall (or can) see the Lord, must not Christ be much more earnestly anxious to make us holy than we can be to be made so? If we do not believe in this earnest anxiety of His, do we believe in His love at all? Have we ever really apprehended it; or has it been merely a tale recited in our ears, which we do not care indeed to contradict, but which has never at all taken hold of, or touched our hearts?

"Ah! what if these struggles to be holy should themselves be in a certain sense a token of unbelief?" What if the poor bird imprisoned in the cage should be thinking that, if it is ever to gain its liberty, it must be by its own exertions, and by vigorous and frequent strokes of its wings against the bars? If it did so, it would ere long fall back breathless and exhausted, faint and sore, and despairing. And the soul will have a similar experience which thinks that Christ has indeed won pardon and

acceptance for her, but that sanctification she must win for herself, and under this delusion beats herself sore in vain efforts to correct the propensities of a heart which the word of God pronounces to be "desperately wicked." That heart,—you can make nothing of it yourself;—leave it to Christ, in quiet dependence upon His grace. Suffer Him to open the prison doors for you, and then you shall fly out and hide yourself in your Lord's bosom, and there find rest. Yield up the soul to Him, and place it in His hands, and you shall at once begin to have the delightful experience of His power in sanctifying."—*Dean Goulburn, D.D.*—"Thoughts on Personal Religion," p. 24.

Soul-Health.

OUR great need as sinners is *life* — spiritual life. Being by nature " dead in trespasses and sins," we need to be quickened by the Spirit of God. Our great need, as those that have been quickened, is the maintenance of *soul-health*. Health supposes life. There can be no health until there is life. But there may be life without health. This is true of the soul as well as of the body.

Have we, as Christians, sufficiently recognised the importance of living in the vigour of *soul-health ?* Have we not thought it enough so long as there has been spiritual life at all? And yet how impossible it is to over-estimate this blessing? Just as the soul exceeds in value the worth of the body, so soul-health surpasses in importance the health of the body. We know the effect of disease on our physical system; how it impairs our strength, takes away the appetite, and destroys our enjoyment of God's temporal mercies. Not less marked are the effects of soul disease. To the prevalence of so much sickness among the members of the Church of Christ may be traced the lack of spiritual power, the want of appetite for the word of God, and the absence of joy and gladness in what Christ is made unto us.

It is a fact, which cannot be controverted, that a large proportion of those who have trusted in Christ for salvation and deliverance from condemnation, are still so enfeebled by spiritual maladies that, instead of being strong, courageous, active, and victorious over the sin that daily assails them, they are weak, timid, desponding, and continually being overcome by the enemy.

But many there are who believe there is a better life for them here on earth than this sad experience of incessant failure. And, blessed be God, many there ·are who are

beginning to live that life! To those who
are seeking it we would say, See that you do
so in God's way, not by works, but by faith.
Not by doubting, but trusting. Unbelief is
the parent disease of all our ailments—it is
the disease that so readily affects us, just as
it is the sin that so easily besets us.

For physical health there are three things
we justly regard as absolutely essential—good
food, pure air, and sufficient exercise. Those
three things, in a spiritual sense, are as essential to the health of the soul.

Let us see how they are provided for us in
the kingdom of God.

First—There is the *food of His word.*
Upon that inspired word the believer must
feed *daily* if he would be strong. " Man shall
not live by bread alone, but by every word
that proceedeth from the mouth of God." How
can the soul of the Christian be in health if
he neglects to take in spiritual nourishment,
or if he habitually feeds upon injurious food ?
And by feeding on the word, we mean not

simply the *reading* of the " daily portion," but a true *digestion* of that which is read. It is only thus that the bone and sinew of our spiritual life are formed. " Thy words were found, and I did *eat* them ; and Thy word was unto to me the joy and rejoicing of mine heart " (Jer. xv. 16).

One of the marks of disease—of the soul as well as of the body—is loss of appetite. When there is no inclination for the reading of the Scriptures, a reluctance for religious conversation, or for anything pertaining to God's kingdom, we have an evidence of spiritual disease. But the word not only satisfies the hunger of the soul, it restores the health that has been lost. " He sent his word and healed them."

Second—*The atmosphere of His presence.* Man subsists upon the air he breathes more than upon the food he eats. He is not always partaking of food, but he is always breathing. Even while he sleeps he breathes. And this is equally true of the soul.

II

We need an atmosphere to live in as well
as food to feed upon. That atmosphere is
Christ's own Presence. In Him we are " to
live and move and have our being." It is, of
course, quite possible for a Christian to get
out of that atmosphere, to cease to "abide in
Him." And then what follows? Just what
would follow if from a pure and healthy
climate a man were to go and take up his
abode in a locality where the air is full of
malaria, or all kinds of noxious vapours.
Disease would be the inevitable result. The
best of food could not of itself alone counter-
act the evil. Most of us are keenly alive to
this, so far as the body is concerned. Would
that we were as careful with our souls !

How can the Christian expect anything but
weakness and disease when most of his time
his soul is breathing the poisonous atmosphere of wordliness ? " But," does some one
ask, "how can I always be in this atmosphere?" " My Presence shall go *with thee*,"
is the answer. In every duty, in every lawful

pursuit, in every pure and innocent recrea-
tion, we may count upon having with us the
hallowing Presence of Christ. The way
which our Heavenly Father has marked out
for us to walk in is the path in which Christ
never ceases to be present. In that path we
may ever breathe the pure air of Divine holiness.

It is, therefore, a vital question when con-
sidered spiritually—"Where do you live?"
Where is it that your soul habitually dwells?
Can we answer

> "In God I have found a retreat,
> Where I can securely abide,
> No refuge nor rest so complete,
> And *here I intend to reside*"?

"He that dwelleth in the secret place of the
Most High, shall abide under the shadow of
the Almighty." Let the soul live in that
atmosphere and he need not fear the "noi-
some pestilence." In "His presence is salvation" from spiritual disease.

Third—*The exercise of our faith*. There

must be some proportion between the amount
of food received and the exercise needed.
All trial is exercise. And the Lord knows
how much of it we need. If He gives us His
word to kindle our faith—for "faith cometh
by hearing, and hearing by the word of God"
—He gives us also the trial to exercise our
faith. "That the trial of your faith, being
much more precious than of gold that perisheth," &c. (1 Pet. i. 7).

And if He feeds us with truth, which com-
forts our hearts, and strengthens our lives,
He will call us to practise what we have
professed to believe. This practice is the
exercise of faith.

Some Christians are sick, not because they
have not the truth, but because their practice
falls so far short of their doctrine. There is
such a thing as spiritual dyspepsia.

We must have the practical carrying out
in the daily life of those principles we hold as
the articles of our faith. We believe, for instance, that the Christian is one who is to be

distinguished amongst other things for the
gentleness and love of his spirit, the truth
and sincerity of his character, the integrity
and transparency of his actions. And we
believe that these are fruits which he is utterly unable of himself to bring forth; that
they are the outcome of Divine Life within;
that it is only as he dwells in Christ, and
Christ abides in him, that his life can thus
become transformed into the image of God's
dear Son. Now these truths are not only to
be held as doctrines, they must be "*translated* into action," as Coleridge says. And
to this end, with the deep conviction of our
own utter helplessness in the matter, we com-
mit our souls to Christ. We yield ourselves
to Him to keep us and work in us. We expect, as we abide in Him, practically to be
able to bring into exercise these very virtues for
which of ourselves we are utterly insufficient.
Let this trust in Christ be true, and we shall
find that our lives, though calm and peace-
ful, will be intensely active. No spiritual

disease arising from a want of exercise, will then assail us; but, as with the Thessalonians, our faith will "grow exceedingly," and the practical manifestation of Christ will abound.

Fruitfulness.

FRUIT is the *final* effort of the tree. It is the witness to life, health, growth, and development, as antecedent conditions. In perfection and abundance fruit is the evidence of the unhindered flow of the sap from the root to the branch—of an adequate supply of nourishment—of a sufficiency of moisture and sunshine. Without these conditions fruit would not be possible.

So when we read of the "*fruit*" of the Spirit let us understand what is meant. There are the offices and work of the Holy Ghost—but this is the *result* of His operation. There is the indwelling of the Spirit—but this is the *outcome* of His indwelling. Not so much that which He introduces, as that which He produces.

The world lays the greatest stress upon fruit

—tangible practical results. But it is not there that *we* must *begin*. If we would "walk worthy of the Lord unto all pleasing, being fruitful in every good work," we must go farther down, we must penetrate deeper, even to the root, the source and condition of all fruitfulness. There must be *life*, and *union*, and *communion*. "Without ME"—said Christ, apart from ME, that is out of fellowship with Me— "ye can do nothing." You may be a child of God, and yet not be living in fellowship with Him who is the source of all fruit. "From ME is thy fruit found." "Being filled with the fruit of righteousness which is by Jesus Christ." Righteousness-fruit is the result of abiding in the Righteousness of One, and having Him formed within.

How much is there in our service which we call fruit which is not fruit at all! External results are not necessarily fruit. A Judas may carry the Gospel and proclaim it, and souls may be saved in consequence. But this would not be fruit *in* the messenger. On the other hand, let the heart be true, let the soul be in unhindered fellowship with Christ, and although no outward results in the way of conversion may be *seen*, God will be glorified because there will be the fruit of godliness *in* the labourer. So the Apostle thanked God on behalf of the Colossians, not because the Gospel brought forth fruit *through* them, but because, as he said, it " bringeth forth fruit *in* you " (Col. i. 6). Fruit *in* the life cannot but be accompanied by fruit *through* the life. The mightiest power for usefulness, is the quiet influence of a life that abides habitually in the secret place of the Most High—right in the centre of all fulness. This is to be "made mighty IN *all might*, according to the power of His glory." Not the least of that fruit which will then be found *in* us will be the " all patience and longsuffering with joyfulness," of which the Apostle speaks in the same passage.

It is the fruit that is the glory of the vine. It was by the fruit of His holy consecrated life that our blessed Redeemer glorified His Father. The perfect response of His spotless soul to the will of His Heavenly Father was the glory that belonged to Him who was God's Vine. But it is not Christ alone we now see; but Christ and His people. Nor is it Christ *with* them merely—but Christ in *union* with them. He does not say "I am the true vine, and ye also are other vines planted in the same vineyard;" but He says "I am the vine, ye are the *branches*." Their life should not be a life *like* His merely, and running *parallel* to His life, but both He and they should be sharers of one and the *same life*. And so His fruit is now to be found on them. "The glory which Thou gavest Me I have given them"—I have given, and *continue* to give them.

But there are practical *hindrances* to our fruitfulness, against which we need to be on our guard. Such as

Want of nourishment. This may be the result of worldliness of spirit. As it was with the " thorny ground " hearers in the parable of the Sower. " The evil here is neither a hard nor a shallow soil — there is *softness* enough, and depth enough; but it is the existence in it of that which draws all the moisture and richness of the soil away to itself and so *starves the plant.*" Are there not many of God's children who are thus, through the " cares of this world, the deceitfulness of riches, and the pleasures of this life, or the lusts of other things," *starving their souls ?* How can they be fruitful ?

Or it may be they are in the habit of feeding upon food which is positively injurious to their spiritual well-being. The solemn consideration that the seed we sow in our hearts and mind produces fruit *after its kind,* should make us very jealous as to the character of the literature, for instance, we are in the habit of reading.

There must be the daily *feeding* upon the word of God. We may read it and yet not feed on it. To feed on it the soul must be hungry and faith must be in exercise. The tree to which the child of God is compared (in Jer. xvii. 8) is not only placed in favourable circumstances, "planted by the waters;" it has to fulfil its own functions by appropriating the nourishment thus provided for it. She "*spreadeth out her roots* by the river;" and so among other characteristics that should mark this tree this was one—she "shall not cease from yielding fruit."

May we know more in our experience of the truth of the text: "Thy words were found, and I did *eat* them: and thy word was unto me the joy and rejoicing of mine heart"! (Jer. xv. 16.)

Want of sunshine. There are some Christians who seem to be afraid of enjoying *all* the rays of the Sun of Righteousness. They are afraid of being too happy. They are like trees on the cold north wall of a garden. The soil is good and the trees are good, but the fruit is scanty and never ripens, because it lacks the warm genial rays of the sun.

Perhaps some of us have not really considered that "joy" is itself a part of that
fruit by which we have to glorify God. There
is nothing to be gained by despondency.
Doubts are no marks of humility; unbelief
is really an evidence of pride. And there is
no cloud that so effectually shuts out the glad
sunshine of our gracious Father's face as the
thick cloud of unbelief. May we never forget
the words of the Psalmist, " Blessed is the
people that know the *joyful* sound : they shall
walk, O Lord, in the light of Thy countenance. In Thy name shall they *rejoice all
the day :* and in Thy righteousness shall they
be exalted."

Faith's Abiding Place.

IN a work of a well-known Scotch divine occurs the following striking observation :—
"To make *the death of Christ a mere refuge-
house for pardons* is to degrade it to the most
selfish end, and to receive the grace of God
in vain. The Lord whom we acknowledge
laid down His life to blot out all the sinful
past; but He rose again, that, in His spirit
of purity and love, He might be our Leader in
the war with sin in every form and degree."*

"The death of Christ a mere refuge-house
for pardons"! Let us not shrink from
the searching thoughts suggested by these
weighty words.

The cross of Christ *is* our refuge for pardon; and to the cross we must look to the

---

* Sermons by the Rev. John Ker, D.D.

last, as the ground and source of the forgiveness of sins. But Christ is more than a
Refuge. He is the *Home* of the soul that
has been forgiven and saved. In Him is
more than forgiveness—in Him is purity.
He is not only the Refuge for pardon—He is
the Dwelling-place for *holiness*. The salvation God has given us is by His Son—first
through His blood, and then *in* His life.
"This life is *in* His Son." He, the Risen
One, is the true element of the saved soul.
Just as the water is the element of the fish,
and the air is the element of the bird, so the
Living, Personal, *Present* Saviour, is the element of the renewed soul. The fish lives
whilst it is in the water; the bird lives whilst
it is in the air; so the believer lives whilst he
abides in Christ.

Have we not too exclusively taken these
words, " in Christ," as referring to our
standing in heaven? We have not sufficiently grasped the meaning of the phrase in
its *practical* bearing upon our spiritual life,

as indicating the sphere in which here on
earth we are called to abide. The very term
" abide " implies a locality — a place. If
abiding is a reality, the place in which we
are to abide is also a reality, though unseen
and spiritual. That place is Christ.

On the cross Christ is our propitiation —
the source of our salvation — the ground of
our confidence. In glory Christ is our standing — our completeness before the throne. In
His spiritual Presence here on earth He is
the Sanctuary of our souls. " The perpetual
presence of Christ is the highest article in
the whole Christian creed. It was no figurative
language that our Lord employed when He
said, ' Lo, I am *with you* always, even unto
the end of the world.' His crucifixion is only
the base of His resurrection, and His resurrection is only the base of His ascension, and
His ascension is only the base of His perpetual presence."* To abide *in* that pre-

* Rev. James Vaughan.

sence is to *live*, in the highest and truest sense.

"In Him" is *peace*—soul-filling and abiding. "These things have I spoken unto you, that *in Me* ye might have peace" (John xvi. 33).

He is above all unrest—all corroding care and anxious fear. If *we* are restless and full of fear, it is because we are not *by faith abiding in Him*, where all is "perfect peace."

"In Him" is *victory*. He is above all powers of darkness. He has overcome every foe. If *we* would overcome we must not seek it by *struggling* to get into the victorious position, but by *faith*, taking our position *in* the Victorious One, overcome "*in* Him." Victory will depend, not upon our attainments—*what* we are; but upon our position *by faith*—*where* we are. "This is the victory that overcometh the world, even our *faith*."

"In Him" is *fruitfulness*. If we would bring forth fruit, we must not seek to do it by vigorous efforts *from self*, but by taking our

I

place *by faith* in Him who is the Vine. "Abide in Me, and I in you." "*From Me is* thy fruit found." "He that abideth in Me " —*i.e.* he who is living in *fellowship* with Me— " and I in him, the same bringeth forth much fruit."

"In Him " is *purity.* He is our sanctification. We *have* Him as our holiness when we abide in Him. God was said to have dwelt in the bush (Deut. xxxiii. 16). The bush was in the fire, and the fire was in the bush. It was holy, not because of anything in *itself*, but because *He* was holy who dwelt in it. So, if we would be holy, we must not seek it as something to be obtained *out* of Christ, but as that which we have *in* Him by faith, and which the Holy Ghost will unfold and reveal to us more and more, as we abide in Him. It is not merely that Christ in heaven is the *Source* of our sanctification, and the Holy Spirit is the Agent who sanctifies us. It is more. Christ *Himself* is our sanctification here with us—the " life-sphere " of the soul. If we would be holy, the first condition is that we be *in Him*, judicially *and* experimentally.

"In Him" is *power*. Not merely has all authority (ἐξουσία) been given unto Him in heaven and in earth (Matt. xxviii. 18), but He is Himself "the Power (δύναμιν) of God" (1 Cor. i. 24.) It is when we are abiding in Him that we are being kept *in* (ἐν) the Power of God through faith (1 Pet. i. 5)—garrisoned as in a fort.

"In Him" is *fulness of supply*. "It pleased the Father that *in Him* should all fulness dwell" (Col. i. 19). To enjoy that fulness we must abide in the place where the fulness *dwells*. It is "*in* Him" that all the promises are "Yea" and "Amen." It is "*in* Christ Jesus" that "my God shall fill to the full all your need according to His riches in glory" (Phil. iv. 19). And it is "*in Him*" that we are "filled full" (Col. ii. 10).

It is not enough, then, that Christ is the refuge of my soul—the place to which I m---

instantly flee when sin overcomes me. I must know Him as the *home* of my soul, where, if I only abide, "sin shall not have dominion over" me (Rom. vi. 14). "Preserved in Christ Jesus" (Jude i). "God is love; and he that dwelleth in love *dwelleth in God*, and God in him" (1 John iv. 16).

The Fountain of Life.

"ALL my springs are in Thee." These words are easily said. But how much is comprehended in that single sentence! The life of each one of us is like a stream—whose waters are ever flowing without intermission, and glide by never to return. Every stream must have a source. To every river there is a spring. " Keep thy *heart* with all diligence, for *out of it* are the *issues* of life." There we have the fountain—the heart—as well as the stream—the "issues of life." The outgoings of a man's heart are his life. Consider what these are. There is the stream of our *thoughts*. What a world there is in our thoughts! How ceaseless is the procession—how varied their character! Vain thoughts, impure thoughts, selfish covetous thoughts, malicious thoughts; and then there are holy thoughts, thoughts of peace, of purity, and love. There is the stream of our *words*. These are sometimes foolish, unkind, untrue. Or they are the words of wisdom, of edification, of grace. And there is the stream of our *actions*. This is seen in the course we follow, the steps we take, the fruit we bear. By these we are to be known.

Now the character of the stream will depend upon the nature of the fountain. Let the spring be impure and the waters will be foul. The source of the evil seen in the life lies in the heart. "*Out* of the heart proceed evil thoughts, murders," &c.

To purify the stream we must begin with the fountain. There are many sincere souls who are working hard at the wrong end. To try to cleanse the stream—the outward life—while the source—the heart—remains unrenewed and impure, is labour in vain.

But heart-work is Divine work. "I, the Lord, search the heart." He alone really knows it. He alone can change it. He alone can cleanse it. And so He says to you and to me, "My son, give ME thine heart." And our prayer should be, "Create in me a clean heart, O God; and renew a right spirit within me." To be able to say truly, "*All* my springs are in *Thee*," we must have Christ formed within (Gal. iv. 19). He is not the *Spring* of your life—that is of your thoughts, words and actions—unless He has full and unreserved possession of your heart. He must be where the stream of your life takes its rise, or the life that you now live will not be the Christ-life. There, in the centre of your being, He must *live*—"Christ *liveth* in me"—in order that all your springs may be in Him.

I may know Him as the fountain of living waters. I may have accepted His gracious invitation: "If any man thirst, let him come unto Me and drink" (John vii. 37). That is, to have Him revealed *to* me as the source of all spiritual life. But I may still need to know Him as the "well of water" *in* me "springing up into everlasting life" (John iv. 14).

In the first the spring is *without*—in the second the spring is *within*. And from this there follows the third stage of experience: the living waters flowing *from* us. "He that believeth on Me, as the Scripture hath said, out of his belly shall flow rivers of living water. But this spake He of the Spirit which they that believe on Him should receive" (John vii. 38, 39).

Is not this the secret of a real understanding of that marvellous passage: "Bringing into captivity *every thought* to the obedience of Christ"? (2 Cor. x. 5).

If it is true that "all our springs are in Him," then there will be perpetual *freshness.* They are "*fresh* springs." No matter how barren and unfruitful the soil, how dark and trying the outward circumstances, we shall have a perennial source of refreshment, a hidden spring of living water welling up within, so that our "leaf shall be *green*" (Jer.

xvii. 8). There will be perpetual *fruitfulness.*
We shall "not cease from yielding fruit."
It will be "the fruit *of the Spirit.*" We shall
be "filled with the fruits of righteousness
which are by Jesus Christ, unto the glory and
praise of God" (Phil. i. 11). It will not only
be fruit but "much fruit" (John xv. 5 and 8).
We shall learn how true it is that all real
fruit comes from Him as the source—"*From
Me is thy fruit found*" (Hos. xiv. 8). There
will be perpetual *cleansing.* The need is constant, but the supply will also be continual.
Christ, in His indwelling Presence, has a
purifying power. If He lives within as the
Spring of our lives, those lives will be mar-
vellously changed—they will be sanctified
and cleansed from those sins and impurities
that formerly polluted them. And there will
be perpetual *fulness.* Those words in 2 Cor.
xi. 8, will be brought home to our hearts with
a deeper, fuller meaning. We shall daily be
more and more amazed at the infinite pro-
visions of grace which we have in Him.

" God is able to make all grace abound toward you ; that ye, always having all-sufficiency in all things, may abound unto every good work."

WHY is the world so thirsty,
　　So restless, ill at ease,
　So careworn with its pleasures,
　　So difficult to please ?
Because the truth it cannot see,
That all " Fresh Springs " must be in THEE !

　Why is Thy Church so weary ?
　　Why does Thy cherished Bride
　Appear so sad and lonely,
　　So far from " satisfied " ?
What once she knew, she fails to see,
That all her " Fresh Springs " are in THEE !

　Why needs she so much urging
　　To work, and love, and feel ?
　Why craves she fresh excitement,
　　To stimulate her zeal ?
She cannot, or she will not, see
That all " Fresh Springs " must be in THEE !

(By the Author of " The Old, Old Story.")

The Believer's Sanctuary.

SANCTIFICATION, considered as an act of God, is presented to us in Scripture in more than one aspect. It means separation *from* that which is evil, and it means preservation *in* that which is holy. In the first we have the negative, in the second the positive aspect of sanctification.

It will help many an anxious believer who is seeking after practical holiness if, instead of being occupied with the *process* of being sanctified, he fixes the eye of his faith on Him who is Sanctification itself—on Him who is the sphere, in which alone the process he so much desires can take place. That sphere or region of holiness is referred to in the Word of God under various names. There is one, especially precious, in the seventeenth of St. John. Our blessed Lord is there praying for His disciples. His petition is, " Holy Father, keep through Thine own name those whom Thou hast given Me." Literally, it is not *through* Thy Name—that is by means of, merely—but " *in* Thine own Name." The name of God—which is equivalent to the Presence of God—God Himself —is here regarded as the sphere of their spiritual life, they were to be *in* His name. And the special attribute, " *Holy* Father," brings before us the thought of the unsullied purity, the infinite holiness, of that place in which they were to be kept.

Hence, the believer is not only separated from that which is evil—he is introduced into that which is essentially pure—he is called into a new element, and therein to have his being—an element which is Divine holiness itself. This is to have fellowship with the Father and with His Son Jesus Christ.

" The holiness of God, then, so soon as we are associated therewith, draws a deep line of demarcation between us and those who live under the dominion of their natural instincts, and whom Scripture calls the world. The term 'Holy Father,' here characterises God as Him who has traced this line of separation between the disciples and the world; and the petition: 'Keep them,' has in view the maintenance of this separation. Jesus begs His Father to keep the disciples in *this sphere of consecration*, which is foreign to the world's life, and of which *God is Himself the centre.* The words, "in Thy name," make the revelation of the Divine character granted to the Apostles *the enclosing wall*, as it were, *of the sacred region in which they are to be kept.*" Such are the words of Professor Godet in his admirable commentary on the Gospel of St. John. How beautifully and clearly they explain the meaning of our Lord's words; and how they help us to understand the nature of a believer's sanctification!

There is a sphere, then, which is entirely separate from the world, and from all that is not of God. We have not to ascend into heaven to find it, it is nigh thee. It is found where the need is felt—in the place of sin's tempting power—here in this world of conflict and of trial. It is a region round which God has Himself placed His own barrier. We have not to erect our own fortifications, or build up our own walls against the evil. To be struggling to do this is to make ourselves the centre of our own sanctification. All that God would have His children to do is to enter into His Stronghold—to be garrisoned within His own Holy Presence—to be strengthened in the Lord and in the power of His might.

Again, as there is safety and protection, so also there is purity and power within the Sanctuary of His manifested Presence. We have not to think of sanctifying ourselves in any way apart from Him who is our Sanctification. Our sanctification is Christ Himself, and as such it is perfect and complete. To be sanctified, in a practical sense, we must know what it is by faith to dwell in Him, to

abide within the sphere of His hallowing
Presence. It is thus that we become partakers of His holiness. Our practical participation of Christ is not perfect or complete, it
must be ever advancing.

Let us not, however, be occupied too exclusively with the process of being transformed,
but rather with Him who is the Author and
Cause of our transformation. It is the office
of the Holy Spirit to reveal Christ to our souls
in all His manifold relations. There is none
more precious to the believer than this special
aspect in which we are now contemplating
Him. Oh to be kept within "the enclosing
wall" of His own impregnable fortress—and
continually to dwell within "the sacred region" of His own sanctifying Presence!

" HE shall be for a Sanctuary" (Isa. viii. 14).

" I will be unto them as a Sanctuary for a
little time" (Ezek. xi. 16).

" Thou shalt hide them in the secret of
Thy presence" (Psa. xxxi. 20). "His presence is salvation" (margin) (Psa. xlii. 5).

RESTING on the faithfulness of Christ our Lord,
Resting on the fulness of His own sure word,
Resting on His wisdom, on His love and power,
Resting on His covenant from hour to hour.

Resting 'neath His guiding hand for untracked days,
Resting 'neath His shadow from the noon-tide rays,
Resting at the eventide beneath His wing,
In the fair pavilion of our Saviour King.

Resting in the fortress while the foe is nigh,
Resting in the lifeboat while the waves roll high,
Resting in His chariot for the swift, glad race,
Resting, always resting, in His boundless grace.

Resting in the pastures, and beneath the Rock,
Resting by the waters where He leads His flock.
Resting, while we listen, at His glorious feet,
Resting in His very arms ! O rest complete !

Resting and believing, let us onward press,
Resting on Himself, the Lord our righteousness !
Resting and rejoicing, let His saved ones sing,—
" Glory, glory, glory be to Christ our King."

FRANCES R. HAVERGAL.

CPSIA information can be obtained
at www.ICGtesting.com
Printed in the USA
LVHW080743021120
670383LV00031B/1402

9 781375 697958